To Earth We Have Returned

Marie Thearose

Dedicated to the Bruised Reeds.

Holy Communion

I loved Jesus so much
I once rescued
communion wafers
from the trash
and sprinkled them onto the earth.

The cardinals feasted on them
through winter.

Years later, holy men put me in the trash.

No one came to my rescue
so
I went back to the dirt.

Compost

The blast from your meteor
ripped flesh from bread
blood from wine.

"Not many of you should become teachers,"
for you will wound instead of heal.

I have stood in the craters of
men who had no high ideals.
They dealt out blows,
but the bruises weren't
fatal to my soul.

Yet you blame me for trusting you.
As you clamor for
admiration and adulation
as you say you know best.

I grind the words from
your sermons into powder.
I mix them with grasses
rotten cabbages
worm-eaten tomatoes
and turn the wheel 5 times each day.
I gather the char from the crater
and pour it in.

—

I have given myself to the earth.
She makes no promises.
She takes away, sometimes cruelly.
She gives, often abundantly.
Most importantly: she never lies.

I open the bin
reach in the dark
and finally,
after all this time,
soil.

In my hands the
only Gospel I dare to know:
what gives death, gives birth,
gives to others
to grow.

The Last Stone

I will not cobble together
a defense of myself
with lines from your holy book.

If the book of the earth
her soil nourishing you
with joy and anguish
could not teach you empathy
what more could I say?

Even Jesus
has to spell it
out for you
in the dirt.

Passed Over

Why should anyone die a sacrifice
when living blood flows in me
poured out and refreshed each moontide?

Why must I drain it from
the slit throats of turtle doves
to cleanse myself for
blood I could not help but spill?

No other fount I know
but my own.

And when this red snow
beneath my legs melts
water and blood
will nourish the earth.

Even

The stones cry out for justice
because when you were
confronted with abuse
you pursed your lips.

Mended Blankets

My roots will go deep
into the earth
where yours rotted.

My fire will refine
and purify
where yours scarred.

I will carry water
to quench the parched earth
where you left a drought

I will fly
where you failed.

Your Lot in Life

When you turn back
to gaze at your corruption in ruins
I won't turn you into a pillar of salt.

You don't deserve to be rendered useful.

=

Yearn

Is it you I miss?
Is it god?
Have I tangled one with the other
until I can't identify the first stitch?
Looking through this glass darkly
does it even make a difference?

I don't crave your love
I found I've never needed it.
But you'll have mine
until the day I die
because I've spent my life
starved for worship.

Does it matter who you are?
Your name, your books, your pantheon?
Do you spill your blood
or should I open my veins?
Who makes the sacrifice
to keep the other sane?

Do you keep me alive in your memory
or are you eternal in mine?
Augustine or Artemis,
does it matter what's divine?
We're all uncertain fools
at the mercy of time.

Innocent

As a child I longed for the God in the Sky
eyes fixed in wonder at
Kentucky trees blanketed
in blue.

The churchmen may have given God
an identity, a book of rules,
but once I knew the name
I lost my innocence.

I've been trying to get her back
ever since.

/They could not tell an orphan
where her mother was
in all of this./

Maybe old temples can be restored.
I'll feel the wind rush
through the Asherah poles.
Maybe the sky can open up with rain
and baptize me new again.

Imputation Part I

How impotent your god's grace
that it could not make you a better man
this side of heaven.

Far More than 95

Since you won't let us in
We're nailing all the evidence to the door.

We're not here for reformation.
We're the revolution.

Heretics over Hypocrites

There's an amethyst on my altar
but I've never cast a
spell as potent as the one
where you looked to the sky with a wink
and were absolved.

Your road is wide, your grace is cheap.
Who knew a god's death was meant
for you to stay the same?
For you to lay the blame
on me
for being angry?

How dare I not forgive you
when God did
after you said the magic words?

I don't cast illusions.
But when I throw this stone
I will shatter yours.

Unwise Men

Cast out of your home a heretic
so I went back to the dirt
burrowed under dry soil
waited for the rain
and slated my thirst on petrichor.

With the water I plunged deeper
past root, grub, bone,
into the crystalline mantle
where my weight shifted the plates
and ripped the ground from underneath
the house built on sand.
And great was the fall of it.

Vienna Immaculata

And in the city where your fear of stones was forged
and your hatred of the feminine divine
a pendant of her form was found
and
she is mine
she is mine
she is mine

Failing Your Daughters

You gave me stones
when I asked for bread.
So I gathered the stones
to use for witchcraft instead.

Only St. Paul

The man who has no use
for the Prophets and the Poets
will see no reason to protect the little child
who leads the Lion and the Lamb.

Saccharine

Yes, I'm bitter.
Like lemon in the ice and sugar.
Like cocoa in the cake.
That which keeps sweetness pleasant
instead of saccharine.

Shadow Side

Don't fear for me.
I'm safer in the darkness
than I ever was
in the light.

Hell

The only evil your creed averted
was harming their bodies.
/Harming their minds
Was enough for you./

Don't you dare hang that on your God's cross.
Don't you dare say it was for art.

Hell hath nothing like me.
I've wrung the fury from its flames.
I'm riding to your gate.

Solstice Wick, Solstice Reed

It's the darkest night of the year
and 13 heretics
are braving it
with smoldering flames
they've kept lit
on their own.
Despite a jealous god's followers
attempts to snuff them out.

Tonight
bruised reeds
bake bread
from their bowed heads.

The Divine Masculine

You prop yourself against the walls of the sea cave
your long legs bent against your chest
your long arms resting on them.

You glance at me with deep set eyes
angular features
a warm smile.

I smile slightly, but,
"I don't want to talk to you."

You give a single nod.
You understand.

We sit apart, together.
We listen to the ocean as it echoes 'round the rock walls.
We see the waves crash against the cliffs and the sand.
We watch the shore receive and lose that kiss
again and again.

A New Beatitude

A bruised he will not break
but he will leave you bent.
A smoldering wick he will allow to burn
but he'll never fan you into flame.

Better the one whose stalk has broken
for her seeds will fall to earth
to bloom again.

Better the one who tastes raw ash
for she will know what it is she really felt
nourished by her grief.

Better to be dust
than kept flickering at arm's length.
Better to fall to earth
than kept bending without becoming.

Memory

You get to forget
I have to remember.
The confidence in your forgetting shakes me.

Then relief, others speak the same words.
You can't gaslight a pride of lions.
the more we roar
the less you can forget.
The more spaces we speak
the less you can hide.
Until, like us,
you have to remember
you have to live
with everything.

Bearing Good Fruit

I've felt more power
healing
transformation
compassion
empathy,
in a few imperfect spells--
myself, a stick, a rock, a candle,
some fresh herbs, a puff of smoke,
flawed gods--
than I ever did
at the mercy of a thousand
thundering doxologies.

Speak

I suffered out loud
To smoke you out.

Double Edged Branch

The rod never spared
so your children will be
polite
well behaved
studious
and distant.

Jacob's Limp

Wrestle with god
wrestle with the idea of god.
Walk away limping
walk away without looking back.
Thousands of steps later
the bruises won't heal.
Thousands of steps later and
you're not even real.

Pomegranates

We can't make you care.
Even though we:
break open our souls like pomegranates
weep tears on the roots of dying oaks
walk this path on broken knees
know every word on the page of this heartbreak
let you drink from our jugular veins.
You ran away
mouths bloodstained and indifferent
trampling roses, singing,
"They know nothing,
and this is only wine on my lips."

Forest Fire

"The devil quotes the Bible,"
your defense against
everything I believe.

Ah, how did I not see
your forked tongue smoking
with words you were not fit to speak?

Land of the Living

From your throne room
of whitewashed tombs
you hand me your decree of exile.

Good.

I've run to the temple
on the outskirts of town
to ask my questions.

Where the oak roots grow deep
where we walk like trees
amidst the hurting on the margins.

Where the real
the radical
work begins.

Adamas/Unbreakable

In my hands there is coal
and it will take years of pressure before
diamonds come spilling from my fingertips.

~.~

As a child I held these hands open.
You grasped them and said
you'd show me the way.
You'd give me the manual
and lay out the path.
And lead me on to places
I didn't want to go.
All the while the coal gathered dust
the light flicked away
and it grew cold
on the shelf.
It was during that time
that you laid claim to me
but you don't get the rest of me.

~.~

I picked it up today
and felt the rough weight of its potential
against my warm palm.

~.~

Good things grow in the gardens of my mistakes
but that doesn't erase the regret.
You can blame me for it all, if that's what
helps you rest in peace.
You can tell the world I didn't have to listen,

if you think that will grant you absolution.

No matter what it is you now say,
I have to walk the path
you were trying to protect me from
because it was wide and open
and it splintered into paths infinitum.
In all its complexity and rich topiary
you thought there was only chaos.
But there is beauty
and freedom.
and yes, chaos

(the lie was thinking you could protect anyone from it).

I thought I'd have to turn back from certain trails
since you had already taken much from me
and they were steep and far too long a road
for a drained soul.

But there is a difference between the hard, necessary work
of surviving the blows,
and the hard, necessary work of coming alive.

~.~

I wrap my fingers securely around the atramental stone
I crack and bleed from the coarseness.
I blister and peel from the heat.
But it is mine to form
and I will not let go
for no man.

Uncertain, Okay

I went to the woods to run back home.
I went to the stones to so I could lay a weight on my heart
that held it in place with comfort
rather than crushing it with rules.

I went to the trees to tell me the old, ancient questions
No more easy answers, no more easy answers,
my soul pleads.

I went to the moss to feel its velvet
comfort my mother's heart.

I went to the streaming waters to remember the oldest
songs, to have them get stuck in my head again,
to drown out the modern hymns.

I went to the sunlight so I could see myself as I truly am.

I went to the animals, so that I could have friends who
expected me to be kind, compassionate, and loving,
but not correct.

When I lost you I went back to the last version
of myself I could remember:
the one who pressed her face deeply into the open bodies of
the fragrant flowers
feeling their plush petals against her flesh
and inhaled.
Daring to hope
but not to know.

In Spirit and In Truth

Certainty and ecstasy were never going to live side by side.
You dove in to find all the words you ached for
but the inkwell never runs dry.
So release your breath, fill cup to brim with wine,
enjoy the dive.

Proof

You ask for a defense of my beliefs. You want a
dissertation on my soul. This cannot be provided.
Spirituality—an abundance of it, a lack of it—is intensely
personal. I hold mine with an open palm to help me live,
not to convert. I will tell you: my soul flutters on
moonlight. I will tell you: the stones and soil give me
comfort. This telling is all I can do. For there is no photo of
my soul in flight under the wolf moon. And the stones and
soil did not write their wisdom.
But if you pay attention you may find your own holy
mysteries. You'll know them because they will make you
better, kinder, stronger, than you were before.

Hope

How corporeal and gossamer.
How relinquished from my grip.
How familiar and foreign.
How fragile and intense.

How like a sanctuary.
How like a risk.
How like a sundrenched waltz
How like an aphotic kiss.

How it could betray.
How it could defend.
How like a fractured dream
bandaged with sanguine ribbon.

Bloodletting

In my dissociative moments I think
I will open my wrists
carve them out like the rivers
that carved the canyons.

From them water will pour out
and carry the heartbreak
the rage, the longing for the past,
the grief over what's been lost
the thousand words I was denied...

they will flow out of me at once
and I will be free.

I do not do this
for the ill mind
can take a hope,
like a hope for freedom,
and turn it into a lie,
a path toward death.

But at least I know
when my mind breaks from my body
it's because my mind believes there's hope
no matter how broken it may be
that I can be free.

Always

I picked up your book in this mourning
and reached the part where you
cursed the fig tree
and set it down in frustration.

How could you, of all people, be so petty?

Then I laid in bed grieving my complicated loss.
Then I realized something I said was true of you.

The hurt was real.
but so was the hope:
for nourishment
What a thing to be dashed!
How utterly human you were
to lash out about it.

So, even in that
you're here with me.

Imputation Part II

"God loves you.
Well, not you.
But the version of you
he has to imagine
is good enough to love."

Oh, friend with jaw dropped
at news of my apostasy
the phenomenal thing isn't my disbelief.

It's that you cannot fathom
why I would want
nothing to do with
that god.

Haunted

No stone I could carry would absorb
all the negativity you gave.
No cords left to cut, no,
I'm left permanently waterstained.
You'll be the flutter in the curtain
that I can't brush off as the wind.
You'll be the flicker of a flame
on the bridge I left smoldering.

Candide

My dream of revenge became a nightmare that left us
forever entwined,
my feet trapped in the cement above your grave,
the one you dug for yourself,
but I handed you the shovel.

And that is a far more frightening thought
than you living this life
without ever feeling an ounce of my pain.

What I've been trying to say,
with every riff on crepe myrtles
with every venomous couplet
is God's name.

I needed you to know everything you did
got in the way.

So, here,
dig yourself a garden instead.

Yahweh.

22786534R00028